DAADI MAA'S DIARY OF SECRETS

TearJerker
Picture Books for Big Kids & Adults

Written by Monita Kumari

Illustrated by Yadnyee Shingre

Be sure to check out Monita Kumari's website at MonitaKumari.com

ISBN 979-8-9884202-0-0
Printed in United States of America
First edition, January, 2024

Cover design by Daulat Ram

To my parents, thank you.
And to my favorite boys in the entire world,
Gaurav, for always believing in me, and
Gautam, for lending me his beautiful handwriting
for Daadi Maa's diary entries.
Thank you,
I couldn't have done this without you!

— Monita Kumari

Within the four pillars of my life,

Mummy, Baba, Sonu and Harvey, the sentiment remains:

"I am because we are" – Ubuntu

— Yadnyee Shingre

Vivek didn't like grapes. It was just his luck that his Daadi Maa grew grapes and made her own raisins. She put raisins in everything. And if that wasn't enough, she pinched him every chance she got. So much that it sometimes felt like she did it just to annoy him. Vivek wasn't sure which one he despised more: the raisins or the pinching.

One weekend, Vivek decided to return the favor by taking Daadi Maa's old diary without her permission.

Stealing was wrong and Vivek knew he'd be in so much trouble if Mom found out, but it was the most excitement he'd had the whole weekend.

He couldn't have stopped himself even if he'd wanted to.

"Have the grapes ripened much?" Mom asked when he got back home. "What did Daadi Maa make for you this time?"

Vivek could never tell when Mom was mocking him and when she was being serious. This certainly was one of those times.

"Daadi Maa pinched my cheeks again and said you were doing a poor raising me. It was horrible!" Vivek complained.

He was seven years old. All this pinching business was for babies. No him.

"And," he continued, "her raisin cake was sour."

When Mom chuckled, Vivek gav her what he hoped was one of his angriest glares, but Mom had already turned away. She didn't even notice h much effort it had taken him to look t mad.

Suddenly, slipping Daadi Maa's diary in his bag without permission didn't feel so wrong any more. Daadi Maa was a mean lady. She was alwa pinching everyone. Really hard. making him eat raisins all tl time.

That night, as Vivek pulled his blanket over his head and turned on his flashlight, his heart beat so hard against his chest, he could almost hear it. Daadi Maa was as sour as her grapes. She was absolutely no fun at all. He couldn't imagine her as anything but prim, proper and strict. She never laughed. She hardly ever smiled, as though a wizard had struck her with his wand and made her forget how to.

Vivek shuddered to think how angry she'd be when she found her diary was missing. There was a slight chance that she wouldn't even notice, he told himself - slight but not impossible. And tonight, Vivek was counting on it.

"Secrets are the best," Vivek whispered softly.

With eager fingers, Vivek opened the diary and turned the first page.

Page 1
Myself Padmavati from inside Varanasi, Uttar Pradesh, the daughter of my mother, Ganga, and father, Shivraj, also from inside Varanasi.

पद्मावती

Page 2
I am learning the very ~~phanny~~ funny language known only as English.

"Funny language i[n]" Vivek muttered, the corn[er] his mouth lifting slightly smile.

He'd heard of Varana[si] he'd never been there. He [didn't] think Daadi Maa had eve[r left] her home in Sonoma, Calif[ornia] to visit Varanasi either. [He'd] have remembered for sure.

The name Varanasi [had a] nice ring to it. It sounded [like a] cool place to grow up. Vi[vek's] imagination was already g[oing] crazy in his head.

He could almost see Daadi Maa's mom milking [the] family cow and her dad going off to the bazaar fo[r] vegetables. Maybe he brought back raisins for her. Perh[aps] Daadi Maa was nice when she was a little girl. On second thoughts, Daadi Maa and nice? Nah.

Vivek flipped a few pages ahead.

Page 6
I am seeing Bhola playing with the son of the Policewala day and day, and I am not liking it.

Page 7
Father is police but son is being a crook. I am hoping Bhola will make the friend cut with him fo good.

Vivek flipped a few more pages.

Page 14
My mother and father are of very poor farming family but we make money here and there to ~~learn~~ educate Bhola and hoping to make him big man in Varanasi.

Page 15
Mother and father having no money for ~~dahej~~ dowry to make the marriage for me after that.

Vivek flung back the blanket and rning on his back, he stared at the ling for a good two minutes. This ldn't possibly be true. Daadi Maa had en wealthy as long as he'd known her, d that was pretty much his entire life. couldn't imagine her being poor. If he ught about it, her grapes weren't that r after all. She actually ran out every e she set up a stall at the farmer's rket.

The more Vivek stared at the ceiling, the more his opinion of Daadi Maa changed. Suddenly, a wave of guilt and shame swept over him. If Daadi Maa found out he'd invaded her privacy, there was no doubt in his mind she'd pinch his cheeks right off his face.

The right thing to do would be to close the diary, put it back where he'd found it and pretend this never happened. But following the little voice of wisdom in his head had never been his strength.

And so, failing to close the diary, Vivek turned a few pages.

Page 24
Bhola is young but strong, why, because he is of a farming family working hard, day and day.

Page 25
Still he is playing day and day with the son of the Policewala, the crook. I be worrying for him but Bhola is not ~~afraiding~~ fearing him. He is not seeing danger.

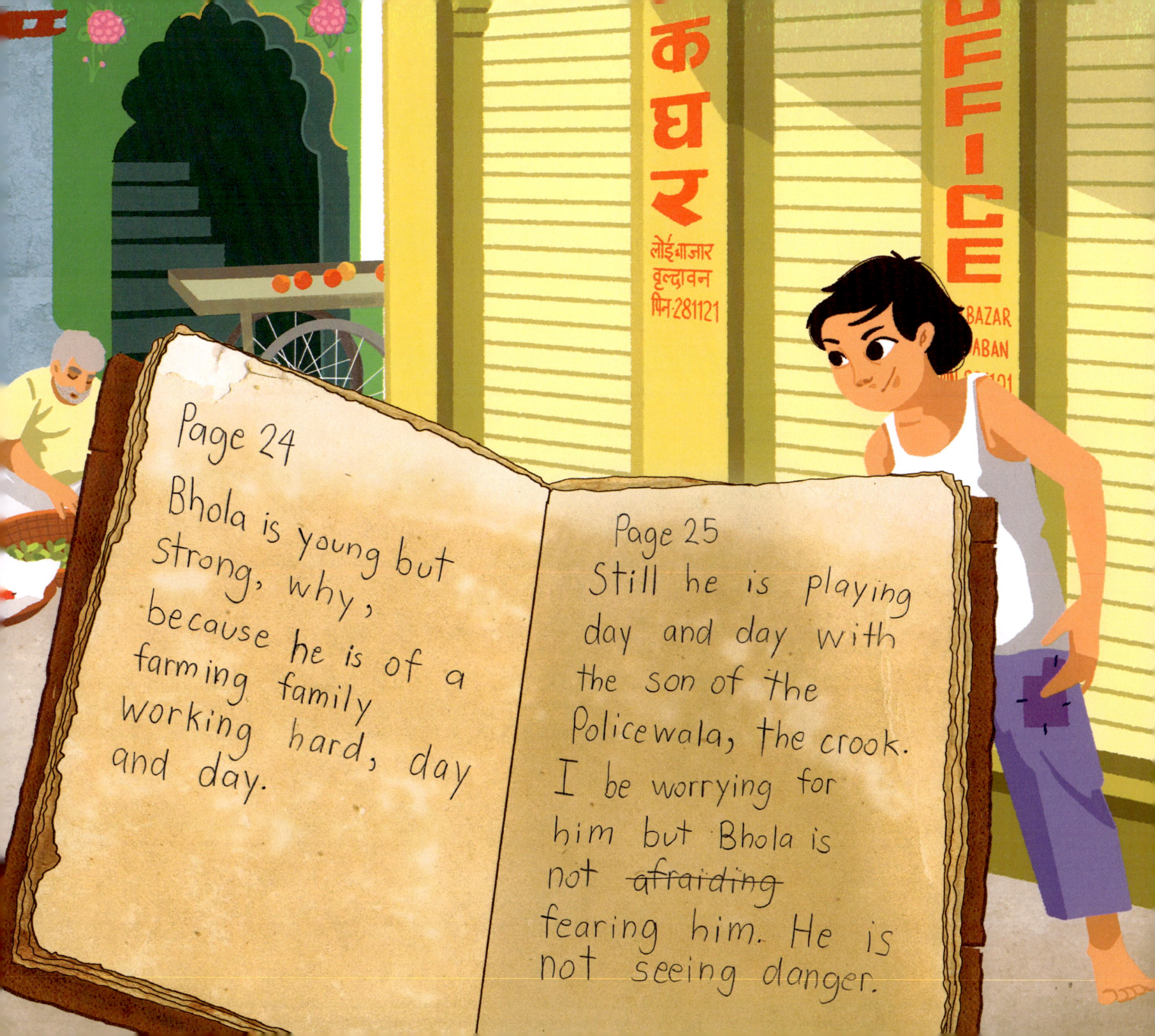

Vivek's fingers trem
as he flipped some r
pages.

Page 28

I am not being friends with the son of the Policewala, why?, because he is bad for all peoples and Bhola also.

Page 29

What to do ? What to do ?

भोला is the best ~~brathar~~ brother.

The suspense was making
Vivek's stomach do a somersault. It
was like reading a real mystery
book. The only difference was that
he knew the main character.

Page 30
Bhola is not having any enemies, why, because he is being a small boy but having a big heart.

Page 31
But today when I am seeing Bhola's everything blue, I am saying to myself, what to do, what to do, but that ~~skoundrel~~ scoundrel son of the Policewala is smiling ear to ear.

Page 32

I am pinching and
pinching and pinching
on his cheeks but I
am not seeing color.

I am pinching only.
No other peoples are
doing.

Page 33

They be too afraid,
but only I am pinching
and pinching his
cheek.

Nothing.

A surge of unease jolted Vivek. He read pages 32 and 33 over and over again, refusing to glance at page 31. Suddenly, all of Daadi Maa's horrible pinching made sense. As long as Vivek winced and complained, Daadi Maa was at peace. Because Bhola had neither winced, nor complained. Bhola had died that day and so had a small part of Daadi Maa.

Vivek sat staring at Daadi Maa's diary for a long time. He couldn't read any further. He wouldn't. Sadness tugged at his heart.

The following weekend at Daadi Maa's house.....

Daadi Maa pinched Vivek's cheek, the hardest yet. "Look how thin you have gone since I last saw you. Doesn't your mother feed you properly? Eat some raisin cake."

Mom released the air from the blood pressure cuff around Daadi Maa's arm, the slight roll of her eyes the only indication she'd heard her. "Your blood pressure is high, Mamma. Your nurse told me you've been throwing your medicine out the window again."

"You're a doctor in your hospital, Netrah, this is my home," Daadi Maa said, pulling Vivek into her lap. "My nurse is a witch. I fired her last night."

"Yes, well, she's going to be back before I leave. And you can't fire her. *I'm* paying her."

"Then you can pay her not to come back," Daadi Maa said, tickling Vivek under his armpits.

"I'm serious, Mamma. You of all people should know how important this is."

Daadi Maa gave Mom a death glare, then they all spoke at once.

"Did you know Daadi Maa was a nurse for twenty-five years?" Mom asked.

"Do you know how naggy your mom is? Nag-nag, nag-nag. Day and night."

"I took Daadi Maa's diary without her permission!"

A pin drop silence followed Vivek's confession for a solid five minutes. Then Daadi Maa pulled him into an embrace.

"I was going to give that rascal to you anyway. It is time I told you about my brother Bhola."

"Daadi Maa, how come you never told me about your brother? Was he murdered? Did *you*... ummm... kill him?"

Mom gasped. "Vivek!"

"No, not physically," Daadi Maa replied. "The police officer's son dared Bhola into doing something that cost him his life. He was a bully and I knew it. I... I was supposed to be watching over Bhola but I -"

"Mamma..." Mom interrupted. "You don't have to do this."

"Keep quiet, Netrah. Let me talk." Daadi Maa sniffled.

Vivek could see how much she was hurting but he could also see how important it was for her to say what she needed to say.

She combed her soft granny fingers through his hair and Vivek braced for a pinch, but it didn't come. The tension exuding from her was like a tangible thing, radiating from her like shards of glass. She gritted her teeth and then pinched the bridge of her nose before swiping a hand down her face.

"Daadi Maa, I'm sorry I wasn't thinking about your feelings and I'm sorry I couldn't hold my questions back, but...," Vivek said softly. "I really want to know what happened that day."

Daadi Maa framed Vivek's face with her tiny fragile hands, keeping him like that until the last possible second. She was silent but her watery eyes spoke volumes. When she couldn't postpone the inevitable any longer, she finally inched her fingers to his cheeks and pinched him gently.

"The truth is that I knew the reality of the situation all along and the reality was that I was treating your dad like my long dead brother."

Vivek frowned a[...] Maa's obvi[...] digression [...] subject of [...] conversati[...] Nobody br[...] Daddy up [...] the sky wa[...] to fall.

"Mamma, Deepak has been dead for five years. I have stopped grieving and I don't blame you for his death. That's the only reality there is to know."

"That doesn't mean I will stop feeling responsible for his death," Daadi Maa countered.

"No, Mamma. That's exactly what it means," Mom said with a loud sigh. When Mom sighed that loud, it meant she was at the end of her wits.

She raised her voice. "How many days, weeks, months and years have to pass before you can trust that I have forgiven you, Mamma? How many?"

A sob escaped Daadi Maa. "This sweet boy didn't get to know his father. I did this to him. I killed his father. Can't you see?"

Mom came and gathered both Daadi Maa and Vivek in a tight hug. "That's not true, Mamma, and you know it. Deepak was your son first before he was my husband or Vivek's father. You have to..."

"We had an argument about Bhola the day he had the car accident. He was complaining that was bad enough that I couldn't forgive myself for Bhola's death but now I was projecting my sorrow by pinching him whenever I got the chance. He was a grown man, for God's sake, he said. He was tired of me treating him like my dead brother, he said." Daadi Maa sniffled. "Deepak was upset when he left the house."

Stuck between them like a sandwich, Vivek looked from one woman to the other and realized both e weeping silently. He wasn't prepared for this. How long should he give them before he said ething? He - like any seven year old - knew nothing about how to comfort crying women.

"Daadi Maa...Mom...I'm here. I'll take care of you both," Vivek said finally because he felt he had to say ething, being the man of the house and all.

Mom kissed the top of his head. Daadi Maa stroked his cheek gently. It didn't go unnoticed by him that hadn't pinched him this time.

For so long, Vivek had whined and complained about Daadi Maa. He wasn't sure when he'd changed opinion but now when he looked at Daadi Maa, he only saw an old woman who was scared of losing ple she loved. Losing her brother Bhola and then Daddy hadn't just shaped Daadi Maa - it had hardened . Now Vivek understood. This wasn't going to make Daadi Maa's raisin cakes any sweeter but at least he a different perspective now.

Vivek pouted his lips and kissed her on the cheek. "Don't worry Daadi Maa, I will take care of you."

Daadi Maa pulled him closer. "Taking care of me will be a lot harder if I break my leg. You've grown so heavy!"

She gave Vivek a gentle shove off her lap and stretched her legs. Mom straightened up and rolled her soggy eyes, but with a smile on her mouth.

The three shared a quick smile. The worst of the sorrows had abated and if miracles really did happen, old wounds would heal too.

Born and raised in Fiji Islands, Monita is a trained medical professional, an artist and an amateur sitar player. She is a descendant of laborers brought to Fiji through the Indenture System from India, so her life has been a colorful mixture of both Fijian and Indian cultures. In her spare time, she likes to observe her backyard birds. Monita lives in California with her family.

For more information, visit her website at MonitaKumari.com

www.ingramcontent.com/pod-product-compliance
Lightning Source LLC
Chambersburg PA
CBRC101537260326
41914CB00023B/1652